William Fairfield Warren

In the Footsteps of Arminius

A Delightsome Pilgrimage

William Fairfield Warren

In the Footsteps of Arminius
A Delightsome Pilgrimage

ISBN/EAN: 9783337270711

Printed in Europe, USA, Canada, Australia, Japan

Cover: Foto ©Lupo / pixelio.de

More available books at **www.hansebooks.com**

IN THE FOOTSTEPS OF ARMINIUS.

A DELIGHTSOME PILGRIMAGE.

BY

WILLIAM F. WARREN, D.D., LL.D.,

President of Boston University,

AUTHOR OF " EINLEITUNG IN DIE SYSTEMATISCHE THEOLOGIE ;" "THE TRUE
KEY TO ANCIENT COSMOLOGY AND MYTHICAL GEOGRAPHY;"
" PARADISE FOUND ; A STUDY OF THE PREHIS-
TORIC WORLD," ETC., ETC.

NEW YORK: PHILLIPS & HUNT.
CINCINNATI: CRANSTON & STOWE.
1888.

PREFACE.

TWO classes of persons, it is hoped, may find pleasure and profit in the perusal of this little book.

The first consists of those who, having read one or more of the biographies of Arminius, have come to feel a keen desire to learn whatever more they may respecting the places and the personal influences in the midst of which so great a life was molded. By such readers each touch of local color in the following pages, each item of antiquarian information, will be accounted precious.

The second class is made up of persons who

have as yet read neither the works nor a biography of this eminent thinker, and who, in consequence of inherited or otherwise acquired misconceptions of his place in the history of Christian teaching, feel no decided inclination to enter upon a personal investigation of his life and times. In the case of these it is hoped that the fugitive and partial glimpses here presented may, if in no other way, at least by their provoking inadequacy, prove an effectual incentive to the perusal of those larger works in which awakened curiosity may find a fuller satisfaction.

As to myself—and in introducing so small and so personal a book I must certainly be permitted to speak with the familiarity and directness of the first person singular—it was early in my theological studies that I became interested in the man whose youthful footsteps are here retraced. For a time I had some thought of preparing a new and complete edition of his works, and of writing a more modern and readable portraiture of his life and character than any we now possess.

During my first residence in Europe, in the years 1856–58, I accordingly visited Oudewater and the other places associated with his life, examining both in public and private archives the few unpublished manuscripts from his pen of which I could find a trace. I conferred freely with the leading scholars of the Remonstrant or Dutch Arminian body, receiving from them courtesies which I can never forget.

One of them, the Rev. Dr. H. C. Rogge, ꞏad a short time before prepared—in Latin, as more current in the scholarly world than the Dutch—a new life of Arminius, the manu-

script of which he kindly allowed me to bring
to America. I also brought certain popular
sketches of the pastoral life of Arminius published by the same, then young, historian,
which a few months later I translated from
the original Dutch, and published in a Cincinnati magazine. The duties of pastorates
quite too heavy for my inexperienced powers
forbade further progress at that period.

In the year 1861 I returned to Europe,
where I remained until 1866. There exacting
duties of a new variety fully occupied my
time, and when, at the expiration of the five
years, I was recalled it was only to be charged
with responsibilities heavier and more multi-
farious than any previously borne. Thus busy
years continually went by, each bringing such
pressing present tasks that literary work of
the historical and critical order became in-

creasingly impracticable. As a natural consequence, the early thought of preparing a new
edition of the writings of Arminius never ri-
pened into a definite purpose, still less into *un
fait accompli.*

In a certain reminiscent mood in the summer of 1880 I penned three journalistic arti-
cles on remembered visits to shrines associated
with the memory of the great Hollandic theologian, publishing them with notes in *The
Christian Advocate* of New York. These ar-
ticles and notes, corrected and enlarged, consti-
tute the substance of the little volume here
presented. Their statements are the more
trustworthy from the fact that they have been
carefully revised by one of the most distinguished of the living representatives of the
Arminian body in Holland, Professor C. P.
Tiele, of the University of Leyden. To the

kindness of this eminent scholar I owe important suggestions, and it is a pleasure, in closing this prefatory note, publicly to acknowledge my obligation and to express my thanks.   W. F. W.

BOSTON, MASS.

CONTENTS.

———◆———

CHAPTER	PAGE
I. In Oudewater	11
II. In Utrecht	15
III. In Marburg	17
IV. In Leyden	19
V. Up the Rhine	23
VI. In Geneva	25
VII. In Basel	27
VIII. In Geneva Again	32
IX. In Padua	35
X. In Rome	43
Notes	46

IN THE
FOOTSTEPS OF ARMINIUS.

I.

IN OUDEWATER.

IT was a charming spring day when I arrived at
Oudewater, the birthplace of the man whose life
and teaching had brought me to Holland. I knew
the wasting Spaniards had left me nothing of the
Oudewater of his boyhood—the lovely "*opidulum
interfluente Isala*"—and yet I wanted to stand on
the consecrated soil which his feet first pressed, and
to feel myself encompassed by the same landscape
and sky-arch between which he woke to human con-
sciousness. There were the same level fields, the
quietly flowing Yssel, trees just like the trees his
wondering eyes first looked upon, streets and lanes
which undoubtedly followed the same lines as when,
tugging at the skirts of his stout Dutch nurse, he first
toddled through them. Among the houses nearly
three hundred years old, it was easy to pick out one

and say, It must have been in such a house as this
that the honest cutler lived to whom, on the tenth of
October, 1560, little James was born.[1] Perhaps it was
on this very site. And here, while yet the child was
scarce beyond infancy, the good father died, and in a
country convulsed and ravaged by civil war left the
orphaned family to contend with poverty. His ashes
doubtless rest in yonder ancient church-yard. Hither
came that good man, Theodore Æmilius, sent of God
to rescue the child of providential calling from the
doom which awaited family and town. It was at
such a door as this that the brother and sister parted
from their youngest brother, and the weeping mother
blessed the boy who could be hers no more. It was
up this very street that the incarnate fiends of Alva
poured, butchering defenseless women and children,
and plying the torch to every human habitation.
Hither, as soon as the tidings reached him up in
Germany, hastened the boy of fifteen from his city
of refuge. Here, alas! the broken-hearted, utterly
orphaned son could find nothing but the now cold
ashes of his father's house covering the cold ashes
of his darling mother, his brother, sister, and other
kin. On what grief did this sky look down that
day! With what heart desolation did that fatherless, motherless, kindredless lad take his last look
at his ash-strewn birthplace, and start out upon the

weary foot-journey of two hundred miles which should take him back to his safe retreat in the mountains of Hessia!

The stillness of the little town, as I approached it, was altogether fitting and helpful. I remember to this day how loud and unexpected a cock-crowing sounded, and how a hammer-stroke coming in above the ceaseless lulling undertone of insect life gave one the impression of a community in which there was but one working member. And how green with rich, dark, vital greenness were the surrounding trees and fields and gardens and road-sides. It was easy to think of a beautiful human life starting in such an environment—hard to think that such scenes of diabolical cruelty as are historically commemorated in painting in the Town-hall could ever have been witnessed in its lovely quietude.[2]

Wordsworth, musing upon the local and personal environment of his own child-life, discerned and gratefully acknowledged the providential ministry of both beauty and terror in the molding and attuning and advancing of his character. Doubtless the same Providence that knew so well how thus to produce a Wordsworth, had purposes of equal wisdom to be fulfilled by these contrasted influences which in childhood fell on young Arminius, partly from nature's peace and loveliness, partly from the mad turbulence

and murderous passions of men.   In riper years he,
too, could well have sung:

> Dust as we are, the immortal spirit grows
> Like harmony in music; there is a dark,
> Inscrutable workmanship that reconciles
> Discordant elements, makes them together cling
> In one society.   How strange that all
> The terrors, pains, and early miseries,
> Regrets, vexations, lassitudes interfused
> Within my mind, should e'er have borne a part,
> And that a needful part, in making up
> The calm existence which is mine when I
> Am worthy of myself!   Praise to the end!
> Thanks to the means which Nature deigned to employ;
> Whether her fearless visitings, or those
> That came with soft alarm, like hurtless light
> Opening the peaceful clouds; or she may use
> Severer interventions, ministry
> More palpable, as best might suit her aim.

II.

IN UTRECHT.

THEODORE ÆMILIUS took his little ward to Utrecht, so straight to Utrecht I went from Oudewater. In what part of the city he lodged those troublesome days, of course, no one can tell. But here is the old cathedral of Saint Martin, under whose arches he certainly must have walked, wondering with a boy's wonderment at an architecture so much surpassing any thing he had seen in his native hamlet. He must have looked upon the frowning fortress of Vreeburg, which Emperor Charles V. had built at the city gate to hold the patriot citizens in check. While here at school he lost his kind foster-father, and was alone in the strange old city. But Providence had not forgotten its charge. Rudolph Snell, a native of Oudewater, and a Professor of Philosophy and Mathematics at Marburg, in Hessia, was in Utrecht on a hasty visit, and finding the lad in destitution, took him to his home in Marburg. Scarce had they arrived at that place of safety when news came that the fiery tide of the war had rolled over quiet Oudewater, and buried home, mother, and kindred forever from his sight. Despite the perils of the undertaking, the frenzied boy would hear of no dissuasion, and started for the desolated fatherland. As we have seen, he dropped his tears of loneliness over the spent pyre of his mother, visited, no doubt, the still identifiable grave of his father, and at last, footsore and weary, but safe from Spanish assassins, arrived again at the hospitable door in Marburg.

III.

IN MARBURG.

A MORE beautiful sanitarium for a bruised and
broken spirit the Father of the fatherless himself
could hardly have provided. Twice I visited this
lovely retreat in the valley of the Lahn, where James
Arminius spent his fifteenth year. In what refresh-
ing contrast to the levelness and uniformity of Holland scenery stood out those wild surrounding hills!
What healing charms for the heart-sick boy were in
these ancient forests and this roaring river! Above
the town, upon the summit of the Schlossberg, stood
the white stone castle of the Hessian margrave.[3]
Under the Gothic arches of its "Hall of Knights,"
only a few years before, the famous conference between Luther and Zwingli had taken place. Doubtless the very table on whose velvet cover Luther
chalked his "HOC EST CORPUS MEUM" was
still to be seen. Melanchthon, one of the members
of the conference, had died the very year of the birth
of Arminius. Here, too, was the new university, the
first one ever founded by Protestants, and in 1575 less
than fifty years of age. Through the kindness of his

2

friend he had not only a home, but also the privilege
of studying in the university. For the improvement
of such opportunities Theodore Æmilius had already
prepared him. Some of his professors could doubtless recall the memorable conference of princes and
nobles and theologians and deputies at the castle in
1529. How eagerly must that youth, destined to become the most famous theologian of his country, have
drunk in these descriptions of the great reformers,
and sought an understanding of their strange doc-
trinal dissensions! At another time with what health-
ful boyish enthusiasm he must have bared his head,
and, with his young companions, waved his cap, as
down through the town swept, with smoking steeds
and armed out-riders and plumed postilions, the margrave's princely equipage! In other moods, of a still
Sunday, under the arches of the beautiful Church of
Santa Elizabeth of Thüringen, how must his heart
have ached over the tragic elements in her life and
in his life, and have turned for comfort to her God
and to his God!

IV.

IN LEYDEN.

NEXT year the lad was in his own country, at the new University of Leyden. To Leyden, of course, I did not fail I go. There I lived over again that wonderful siege which our own Motley has so vividly depicted. I recalled the noble choice of the heroic citizens when, in recognition of their bravery, Prince William of Orange offered them either exemption from taxation or the establishment of a university in their city. I saw in imagination the memorable civic and academic celebration at its inauguration, the ingenious symbolic figures and groups which represented the different faculties in the grand procession, the enthusiasm of the newly emancipated nation rejoicing in its partial deliverance from a tyrant's power. I wondered not that, the news of all this reaching our refugees at Marburg, young James of Oudewater should yearn for his native land once more, and that, at the opening of the October term at Leyden, he should be found enrolled among the students.

Here, in this walled and moated town—the most

ancient in the kingdom—for six years he pursued his studies. In Bertius, a reformed clergyman of Rotterdam, God had given him a new friend and patron, who provided for him as a father. And here stands to this day not only the very building in which Arminius pronounced in later years his masterly oration on the "Priesthood of Christ," and in which he taught theology, and in which he was inaugurated with imposing ceremonies as *Rector Magnificus* of the university, but also the older structure, the expropriated nunnery of Saint Agnes, the *Falyde Bagynen Hof*, occupied by the university from the day of Arminius's arrival till April 16, 1581. Here the lad was taught Hebrew by Rennecherus; theology, philosophy, and the liberal arts by Fengeræus, Drusius, Danæus, and others.[4] Here, after 1577, he studied mathematics and astronomy under his dear old friend, Rudolph Snellius, at that date called to a chair in Leyden. Here, in the ancient nunnery, the library of the university still remains. Up and down these very steps the boy student skipped daily three centuries ago, out of these windows he looked, under this roof he went in and out. Here is the very room, though we know not which, where crusty Professor Donellus lectured, and who, when the university was moved over the Rapenburg to its present quarters, refused to go with it, and continued business "at the

old stand." Here are the old churches with which
the boy must have been familiar—Saint Pancras, built
in 1280 ; the cathedral of Saint Peter, dating from
1112, in which his own ashes were one day to rest.
Who can tell how many times, with fellow-students
of classic history, he climbed the " Burcht," the ruin
of an ancient castle in the center of the town, and recalled the far-off years of the first Christian century,
when, according to a dubious tradition, Leyden was
the *Lugdunum Batavorum* of the Romans? Rem-
brandt and the other great artists of Leyden birth,
who have done so much to immortalize Netherlandic
art, were not yet born, but in the old *Stadhuis* there
is still a " crucifixion " by Engelbrechtsen, on which
young Arminius must have gazed with admiration.
Barren and plain must have been the new Senate
Hall of the university upon its first occupancy in
1581 ; now it is adorned with portraits of the professors from the earliest to the latest deceased. Niebuhr,
recalling the illustrious men who have here labored,
affirms that no spot in Europe is so memorable in the
history of science as this same venerable hall. In
those years young Arminius little knew in what celebrated company his own portrait would one day hang
upon those walls ; still less that, more famous than
any Salmasius or Scaliger or Boerhaave or Grotius,
his own name was, three centuries later, to be the

loadstone to draw pilgrims across continents and seas
to visit the shrines of his nativity and life-work.

The little we know of Arminius as a student in
Leyden is very trustworthy, having been reported to
us by a fellow-student who lived under the same
roof, and perhaps occupied the same room—a son of
Bertius, his patron. From his account it is plain
that the young man of Oudewater commanded the
highest respect both among students and professors.
His early bereavements had not rendered him morbid
and gloomy. Under the influence of the kind friends
whom God had given him he developed a bright and
genial character. With chosen companions he cul-
tivated the muses of authorship. He wrote poetry
as well as prose. And such were his gifts and graces
and scholarship that, as the six years drew to their
close, the authorities of the university made such
representations to certain authorities of Amsterdam that these decided to assume the expense of
sending the promising young *magister* to Geneva, in
Switzerland, then the seat of the most famous theological school in the whole Calvinistic world. With
him we turn our faces southward, ascend the storied
Rhine, exchange the dunes and stagnant canals of
Holland for the cascades and torrents and wild gran-
deurs of the distant Alps.[6]

V.

UP THE RHINE.

THE experiences of young Arminius on his journey up the long Rhine valley in 1582, and on his return down the same in 1586, are wholly left to our imagination. How often in ascending and descending the storied stream did I wish he had left an itinerary! We can only conjecture the historic spots he stopped to visit, and the emotions which were called out by the castled steeps, the vine-clad terraces, the ancient towns, the smiling vales, the picturesque villages and imperial cities above Cologne. The best help toward a reproduction of the travel and of the sights of that time which I could obtain was the diary of Wolfgang Meyer, one of the members of the unhappy Synod of Dort, who, some thirty years after the tours of Arminius, made, and described with conscientious care, his downward journey from Basel to Dordrecht. The curious old book is now before me, but to attempt, by its aid, to follow Arminius through the keen experiences which must have been his on the way from Leyden to Geneva would require more time than we can command. Besides,

the emotions of a highlander descending that historic
water-way from the beauties and the memories of
the Upper and the Middle Valley could never repre-
sent the emotions of a lowlander making for the first
time the ascent.

VI.

IN GENEVA.

WITH most tourists arriving in Geneva thoughts of Calvin dominate all others. As for me, I wanted to avail myself of the associations of the place, not merely to live over again the times of Calvin, but also to enable myself to revivify to mind and imagination the times of Calvin's great disciple, Beza, and those of Beza's greater disciple, Arminius. Here the question first dawned upon me, whether, if Arminius's calling had not led him to become the greatest theologian of his generation, he would not have become its greatest philosopher? No one can patiently investigate the hints and intimations which throw light upon the character and progress of his philosophic opinions and studies, without seeing that he was in a fair way to anticipate the work and the fame of that later Leyden thinker, "the father of modern philosophy," Des Cartes. Already in his twenty-first year when he arrived in Geneva, he had mastered not only the scholastic philosophy of the day, of which the chief corner-stone was Aristotle, but also the writings of the leading critic of that system, Peter Ramus (Pierre Ramee), whose graduation thesis was this proposition: "All things whatsoever Aristotle hath said are false." His fame as a master in these matters had reached the city before him. Soon after entering the university, at the urgent and repeated request of fellow-students, Arminius agreed to give, in his own lodgings, a few Latin lectures upon philosophy. He began, but such was the sensation they created that, according to his biographers, the regular professor of that chair invoked the protection of the faculty, and Arminius was directed to desist from his private instruction or withdraw from the institution. The fame of the University of Basel (Basle), beyond the Jura, being just then in the ascendant, he chose to withdraw for a season, and to betake himself from French to German Switzerland, from the valley of the Rhone to the valley of the Rhine.[6]

VII.

IN BASEL.

BEFORE me as I write lie twelve beautiful photographic views just arrived from home-like old Basel. How vividly they recall to mind the impressions of my first visit to that city of royal name! Kindly introduced by letter of the venerated Tholuck to Professor Hagenbach, I was compelled to receive attentions and courtesies embarrassing in their abundance and heartiness. The genial professor insisted on being my *valet de place*, and under his guidance how keen was my enjoyment of the antiquities of the city! Alas! in like manner as we stood by the grave of Arminius's learned compatriot, Erasmus, and talked of the significance of his heraldic motto, "*Terminus,*" so men are already standing above the graves of both Hagenbach and Tholuck, and discussing the significance of the watchwords of their lives and works. From each, happily, I have treasured mementoes, in works written, inscribed, and presented by their own hand. How I wished that the antiquarian lecture which Hagenbach permitted me to hear him deliver in the university had only been upon "Arminius and

the faculty by whom he was instructed in Basel in
the winter of 1582–83 ! ''

At the date of Arminius's sojourn here Erasmus
had been dead less than fifty years. Both had spent
boyhood years in Utrecht ; both must have played in
the meadows of Gouda, and admired the *Groote Kerk*
of Saint John ; both were born in October, though
nearly a century apart ; both fell on troublous times,
and coming to Basel strangers were received as
friends. As I paced the pavement of the ancient
cathedral, under which Erasmus was laid with hon-
ors by the grateful city, and as I trod thoughtfully
up and down the shady terrace adjoining, and looked
down upon Klein-Basel beyond the river and drank
in all the lovely view, I could but think that young
Arminius sometimes turned hither his footsteps and
thought tenderly of his gifted countryman, and wondered whether the same shady terrace was not a favorite resort of his in those last years, when torturing
gout had prohibited extended walks for exercise.
This at least I knew : that I was standing where the
young Netherlandic student must often have stood,
and was looking far down on a stream which he could
not forget emptied part of its Alpine waters into the
far-off Northern Ocean through channels that passed
through dear old Utrecht, and yet dearer, older
Leyden.'

The Buxtorfs, who later gave such fame to Basel in respect to Hebrew learning, and who were also a Nether-Rhenish, if not a Netherlandic family (*Bockstrop*), were not yet here. John, the father of them all, a "Christmas child," was four years younger than Arminius, and at this very time was studying at Arminius's old retreat, the University at Marburg. He came to Basel to continue his studies the year of Arminius's ordination—1588. From this place, on learning of Arminius's death, he wrote memorable words of eulogy.[s]

Only thirteen years before the visit of Arminius, Pierre Ramee, then perhaps in the zenith of his fame, resided for some months in Basel. He lodged with Catherine Petit, the very woman with whom John Calvin had lodged in the same city at the time when he composed his immortal *Institutes*. With what eagerness must Arminius have sought out the house doubly enriched by such associations!

He can hardly have failed to make the acquaintance of James Meyer, pastor of Saint Albans, and assistant pastor at the Minster. This man was of famous ancestry, and his wife, Agnes, was a daughter of the reformer Capito, and of the more famous and brilliant woman, Wibrand Rosenblatt, who was successively the wife of Keller, Œcolampadius, Capito, and Bucer. If Arminius occasionally spent an evening with them, he doubtless saw the five-year-old boy, Wolfgang, the future delegate to Dort, to whose journey down the Rhine we have already alluded. In his eightieth year this cathedral preacher preached a funeral sermon over one who had suddenly died, taking for a text the passage, " As the tree falleth, so it shall lie." At the close of the discourse he fell suddenly backward, and died himself in the pulpit.

The dean of the theological faculty at this time, and apparently the leading spirit, was John James Grynæus. He was Professor of Sacred Literature. With Arminius he was delighted. When every other student in his class was posed by some difficult question, he loved to throw himself back in his stout chair and cry, "Let my Hollander answer for me!" When his Hollander left the university to return to Geneva, in 1583, Grynæus gave him a beautiful letter of commendation "To all pious readers," which fortunately has been preserved.⁹

Grynæus was not the only one to receive a favorable impression of young Arminius. It is a singular proof of the young man's natural and evident leadership that in the spring or early summer of this first and only year of his residence the faculty of the university should have requested him to deliver a public course of lectures before the students of the university. It seems to have been a kind of providential recompense and offset for the suspicious and churlish action of the faculty at Geneva. He consented, and acquitted himself so handsomely in a course upon the Epistle of Paul to the Romans that the faculty tendered him an immediate promotion to the Doctorate in Sacred Theology. This he modestly declined on the ground of his youth, and the way being now open to return to Geneva with honor and fresh commendation, he did so, and, once re-established there, he soon became almost as great a favorite with Beza as he had been with Grynæus.[10]

VIII.

IN GENEVA AGAIN.

A T Geneva I was in time to enjoy the hospitalities of glorious Merle d'Aubigné. Alas! over his life, too, the heraldic motto of Erasmus has since been written. In far less than three centuries students of antiquated histories of the Reformation will probably search as vainly for any relic or trace of his residence here as I did for traces of the sojourn of Arminius. More emphatically than we can well realize " one generation goeth and another cometh." Happy for him on whose marble tablet, as on his at Coligny, in place of "died," it may be written, "*Rappellé à Dieu.*" [11]

Here two scenes particularly impressed themselves upon my imagination. Were I a painter I could reproduce them again in every line and shading. The one was, *Arminius at the grave of Calvin;* the other was, *Arminus on the spot where Servetus was burned.*

It was natural, and only natural, that at times my fancy should busy itself in reproducing the outer life of the student I had followed so closely, should

picture him in the well-filled lecture-rooms of Beza,
Faius, and Casaubon; in his student-chamber poring
over his well-worn Greek and Hebrew Testaments;
in his occasional recreative boat-ride on placid Leman;
in his Saturday walk to cool Salève; in his vacation
tours through Chamouny and over the Tête-Noire;
in his Sunday devotions under Saint Pierre's historic
arches—but evermore my hurrying thoughts would
come back to Calvin's grave, and say, " Yes, here he
must have stood;" and to that Aceldama of Servetus, and repeat, " Yes, here, right here, he
must have stood also." In the presence of such
pictures what impertinences seemed the modern
reminiscences of Rousseau and Voltaire and Byron
and Gibbon, which guide and guide-books were continually thrusting upon me![12]

But young Arminius is still hungering for knowledge. He has completed his studies in the chief
university of the Calvinistic world. He has won the
high esteem and honor of famed men. But before
he can return forever to the far-off lowlands on the
North Sea he must hear the illustrious Zabarella, of
Padua, the foremost living lecturer of the world on
the principles of Aristotle. He who had been ac-
cused of undue attachment to Ramée now shows his
grand docility of nature and catholicity of spirit by
setting out from the city where he first drew this

3

accusation upon himself, and seeking beyond the
Alps, in papal Padua, the latest utterances of con-
temporaneous philosophy.[13]   In the company of a fellow-student—Adrian Junius, a student of law, afterward an eminent member of the Netherlandic Senate
—he makes a prosperous journey across the Alpine
passes, and reaches his place of destination.

IX.

IN PADUA.

SO I went to Padua. In less than half an hour after my arrival at the railway station I was in the vast library of the ancient university, elbow-deep in its manuscript and printed archives.[14] My curiosity had long been piqued to find out something about this Jacobo Zabarella, the philosopher who, right upon the heels of the Reformation, could draw Protestant students by scores over the high Alps to attend a Roman Catholic university. What was it in his teaching which made young Arminius feel he must sit at his feet before he could return to serve his generous patrons, even though there was not time to secure their previous permission? No writer on the life of Arminius had ever given me the slightest satisfaction. Now, on the very ground, I would see what I could find out for myself.[15]

The task was not altogether simple. First I lighted upon old Francisco, first of note in the family, later Archbishop of Florence, cardinal, and once almost elected a pope. But he belonged too far back, and, as an ecclesiastic, could not, of course, be supposed to

have a son Jacobo, or a son of any other name.   Then,
to my bewilderment, I investigated other representatives of the family, until it appeared that there had
been no less than eleven Zabarellas professors of law
in Padua.   At last, in the ancient histories and dis-
courses of Antonio Riccoboni, Giacomo Tomasini,
Giambattista Contarini, Giuseppe Vedova, Carlo Pa-
tino, Francisco Maria Colle, I got upon the trail of
Jacobo and found my feast.   His complete works, if
I rightly remember, were not in the collection, but I
elsewhere found the titles of them all.   I learned
that the distinguished lecturer was a native of the
city, born September 5, 1533; that he was a *magister*
at twenty, Professor of Logic in 1563, and of philosophy from 1578 till his death in 1589, three years
after the coming of Arminius.   He evidently wielded
a powerful influence outside of the academic sphere.
He was employed by the city in a very important ne-
gotiation with the Venetians, and discharged his duties so satisfactorily that, in addition to large pay to
him, the government voted from the public treasury
one thousand gold ducats as a dowry for his youngest
daughter.   Emperor Maximilian created him a *Comes
Palatinus*, and Emperor Ferdinand afterward made
the high distinction hereditary in the family.   The
king of Poland tried to secure him by large offers of
money and honor, but in vain.   The auditoriums of

the university could not hold the students who
thronged to hear him. As to his personal looks my
authorities disagreed. Tomasini represented him as
positively good-looking— "*spectabilis vultu ;*" but
elsewhere I read that in the *Imperial Museum His-
toricum* he was represented of a "*finstern, wilden,
und gemeinen*" expression! Weeks afterward, one
sweltering day in Paris, in the National Library, I
succeeded in unearthing the aforesaid *Museum* and
the truly sinister likeness. I also succeeded in making in my pocket-book an even more unflattering
pen-and-ink copy of it. His good wife, Elisabetta
Cavaceja, would certainly decapitate me could her
ghost materialize long enough to get a glimpse of
what is at this moment probably the only attempt at
a likeness of her illustrious husband in the New
World.

Zabarella left six sons and three daughters, for all
of whom he is said to have constructed horoscopes.
For, like Galileo, this greatest Aristotelian of his
generation was a devout believer in astrology. Just
before his death he pointed out to his hearers the
malign star under whose fatal influence he predicted
he should fall. The funeral eulogy of Riccoboni is
still extant. The professor's eldest son, Julio, became a famous man, and from an entry in an old
book of annals, under the year MDXCIV, I inferred

that in the Faculty of Arts the father must have been followed by a Jacobo, Jr., who made things lively for his colleagues.[16]

Anon I wandered through the city. Yonder on the north lay the calm Euganean Hills, touched by the waning lights of an Italian day. How familiar must have been that lovely sky-line to the eye of the young lowlander, who knew that in a few months more he must bid an eternal farewell to hill and mountain scenery! Did he not once and again scale their picturesque heights, and visit the last residence and the tomb of Petrarch? Did he not sit in the poet's chair, and study on the walls the frescoes of the singer and of his Laura? Did he not go to the balcony, and gaze out upon the sweet scenery on which Petrarch loved to gaze two hundred years before? Did he not catch some soft poetic mood as he lingered and gazed, and gazed and lingered, in the witchery of that soft Italian landscape? Did not the sand dunes of Holland and the decrees of Calvin come to look terribly prosaic and repulsive in this soft, rich, almost voluptuous, light? Came there not a vision to the young man, who long before had felt poetic stirrings—a vision of a life of freedom, love, song, enjoyment of the beautiful? Came there, then, not one thought of duty which was irksome, one galling recollection of his contract with the kind but dull and stolid burghers of the now expectant Amsterdam Senate? Along with the bitter realization of the dependence of his whole orphaned life so far, woke there not a dream of what it would be to claim for himself his time and powers—to sing immortal sonnets, like Petrarch, at the feet of Laura; to be an artist over yonder on the Arno; to inaugurate a new philosophy, and, like honored Zabarella, draw all young Europe to his feet? Ah, James, history tells no such tale on thee; but if up yonder in Petrarch's balcony, gazing by the half hour out over the great valley, thou knewest nothing at all of such an experience, surely better angels attended thee than are vouchsafed to most.

Zabarella was buried in the famous church of Saint Antonio di Padova. To this I hastened. The tomb of the philosopher interested me, but less than that of the gentle saint to whom the fane belonged, and whose child-like soul was so full of love to Jesus Christ and of the love of nature that he talked of redemption to beast and bird, and preached to fishes in the brooks, wishing in all literalness to preach the Gospel to every creature. There in his silver shrine, beneath an altar fair with carved marble and rich pictures and burning tapers, slumbers in peace and honor the mortal part of this humblest, and therefore greatest, historic representative of a redemption

strictly universal in God's purpose. And as I saw a
reverent peasant drop upon his knee and press a kiss
upon the bright silver surface, and utter a word of
prayer or thanksgiving, I almost followed his exam-
ple, partly from the love I bore to quaint old Anthony, but more from the realization, which just then
suddenly came over me, that here in his youth the
great historic Netherlandic champion of the unlimit-
edness of Christ's atonement must have acquainted
himself with Anthony's life, and must, unconsciously,
have received from it—who knows what impression?
Thenceforth, as a match-piece for my picture of *Arminius at the grave of Calvin*, I hung up in the
gallery of my imagination *Arminius at the shrine
of Saint Anthony*.

Again I was in the streets. They were growing
still, as evening deepened into night. All new things
looked dim and old. I seemed to be walking the
streets of an older Padua, three hundred years agone.
A little way before me I seemed to see two young
men in lively conversation. They were in student
garb, with broad-brimmed hats and robes of black.
The tongue in which they spoke so eagerly was Latin,
and as, aided by the growing stillness of the city, I listened I discovered that the speakers were two young
men whom Zabarella had drawn to Padua, the one over
the high Alps, the other over the Apennines. The

one was born by the cold North Sea, the other on
the banks of the yellow Tiber. Here at the feet of a
common master they had met, and learned to know
and love each other. And just now the youth of
Rome was descanting upon the wonders of the seven-
hilled city; upon its venerable antiquities, upon its
art, upon its history, upon its great Saint Peter's,
now in process of construction, grandest temple of the
Christian world. Suddenly they paused at an ancient
door-way, exchanged their friendly good-nights, and
parted—the Roman youth to mount to his chamber,
the other to pursue his longer way to humbler
lodgings.

The latter I followed as under some strange spell.
Presently he stopped short upon the pavement, and I
heard him exclaim to himself, "James, thou shalt see
Rome. The trusty feet which in boyhood bore thee
safely from Oudewater to Marburg can bear thee from
Padua to Rome. Thou shalt see the splendors of the
world's metropolis. Thou shalt face for thyself its
'Mystery of Iniquity.'"

My draped figure vanished; but as I came to the
public square of the Prato, and seated myself in the
deserted silence, I soon had other visions. I saw
Arminius arranging with Adrian Junius, his com-
panion, for their farther journey. I saw Count Zabarella, the illustrious, give him a letter of specially

cordial introduction to Bellarmine, not yet cardinal, but greatest of theologians in the Roman Church. I saw the professor playfully, and yet not by any means altogether playfully, in parting, exhort his young Calvinist to improve the opportunity to make his submission to the Holy Father, and to come back into the bosom of the only true Church. I saw the youth playfully, and yet not by any means altogether playfully, produce the Greek Testament and Hebrew psalter, which history tells us he read daily in all his Italian journeyings, and point his honored professor to that talisman. I saw him bid farewell to Padua forever; saw him take his way down through fair Ferrara, full of Tasso; on to famed Bologna, home of learning; over the wild Apennines to Florence in its Medicæan splendor; on to Perugia and the seats of old Etruria's prehistoric civilization; on past Thrasymene's storied lake and Terni's matchless fall; on, till all the splendors of the Eternal City lay beneath the raptured gaze of Oudewater's child of destiny.

X.

AT ROME.

ANON I was myself in Rome, and alone, high in the Capitoline tower, I looked silently down on all that had charmed Arminius's eye and fired his Netherlandic pulses. And I seemed to see him enriched with mental pictures of surpassing beauty, laden with new knowledge, broadened with cosmopolitan sympathies, the narrowness of his early education insensibly outgrown, as now from the Porta del Popolo he departed from the world's metropolis. I saw him as on the northern hills he turned to take his farewell look at all that loveliness and glory. And there I blessed him. In my heart I said: " Go, chosen child of Providence! Go without one backward look, one brief regret. God hath grand work for thee. From the hour of birth his hand hath been upon thee. Thou wast suffered to be fatherless and motherless only that thou mightest be the more completely his. To fit thee for thy providential calling he hath taken thee from land to land, and given thee the best wisdom of the world. And thou hast been found faithful. Docilely hast thou learned each lesson and treasured every inspiration. In the balcony of Petrarch, thy *Mons Tentationis,* thou didst triumph. Here in the palaces of pope and cardinal thou hast not yielded to their blandishments. Forward, then, not backward, bend thy gaze. God is with thee. I see thee welcomed to thy native land; see thee the most celebrated preacher in a mighty city whose commerce fills the world; see thee first doctor on the immortal rolls of Leyden; see thee the husband of a new Saint Elizabeth and father of happy children. Beyond these things I see God using thee to liberalize a nation's Church; yea, more, a Church of nations— using thee to strike off from both the absurd, the blasphemous limitations which narrow dogmatists have placed on God's impartial and exhaustless love. I see thy leavening word permeating the world from generation to generation, until from the ends of the earth reverent pilgrimages shall be made to thy resting-place, and millions love to do thee honor." [17]

Two centuries and a half after the departure of that precious youth from the Porta del Popolo, President Wilbur Fisk, the saintly head of the first Arminian university in the world, and an honored representative of millions of American Christians,

was bowing at the burial vault of James Arminius
in the cathedral of Saint Peter at Leyden, and all
my. Roman benediction and prophecy had come
true.

———

Et nunc paterno sidus additum templo
Deum precaris, det gregi suo lucem
Hic quanta satis est, hac det esse contentum;
Det non loquentes sua reperta doctores;
Det consonantes semper omnium linguas,
Aut corda saltem; præpotente vi flammæ
Caliginosas litium fuget sordes;
Ut spiret unum tota civitas Christi,
Vitamque terris approbet, fidem cælo.
—Hugo Grotius.

NOTES.

[1] THE credit of determining the exact day of the birth of Arminius is due to the learned Arminian historian and divine, the Rev. Dr. H. C. Rogge, Librarian-in-chief of the University Library, Amsterdam. Students of Dutch history in this period will find his work in three volumes, entitled *Johannes Uytenbogaert en sijn Tijd* (Amsterdam, 1874), of great value.

[2] At the date of Arminius's birth not a Protestant sermon had yet been preached in Oudewater. His baptism must have been at the hands of the parish priest, and before an altar still adorned with pictures and crucifix. Down to his sixth year no wandering herald of the reformed faith had invaded the province of Holland. That year came the first, as plain and heroic a man as any itinerant or local preacher that ever invaded a staid New England town. His name was Jan Arents, and he was a basket-maker by trade. The following year, 1567, he and the future father-in-law and the future wife of Arminius, then a young girl, were compelled to flee the country to save their lives. Their flight by water to Emden was one of the most romantic episodes in the history of the Dutch Reformation.

[3] The castle still occupies its ancient site. For some years it was used as a common penitentiary, but an enlightened public spirit has rescued it from so ignoble a service, and provided for its preservation as a precious historical monument. The "Rittersaal," in which the memorable disputation took place, has been restored and decorated according to its ancient

style, and in other parts of the building the state archives of the Prussian Province of Hessia are now preserved.

⁴ The following were the first theological professors at Leyden: Guilielmus Feugeræus (Feugeray), the first rector, 1575–79; Johannes Bollius, only one year, 1577–78, studied at Louvain ; Hubertus Sturmius, 1579–83. studied at Heidelberg; Lambertus Danæus, 1581–82, studied at Geneva; Johannes Holmannus, 1582–86. At the opening of the university in February, 1575, the elder Ludovicus Capellus was present under appointment as Professor of Theology, and delivered his inaugural oration; but he left soon after, probably without delivering a single course of lectures, to return to France. It is pleasant to associate Arminius and his academic *alma mater*, even thus distantly, with the later Ludovicus, of Saumur.

⁵ A comparison of the archives of the two universities shows that Lambert Daneau (Danæus), after serving as Professor of Theology in Geneva 1573–81, filled the same office in Leyden 1581–82. It is only natural to suppose that he may have exerted some influence to bring about the sending of Arminius to Geneva. In the history of theological encyclopedia and methodology Danæus is famous as the first writer to treat Christian ethics as an independent science. As in 1582 he returned to Geneva, Arminius may have enjoyed his company on the journey.

⁶ The above is the sole reason given by the biographers of Arminius for his removal to Basel. I cannot help thinking, however, that the feeling of the faculty against him has been grossly exaggerated. The "Spanish" professor, to whom the younger Brandt ascribes the beginning of the opposition, can be no other than Petrus Galesius; but the official records of the university show that he did not become a professor at Geneva until a year after this time. The personal relations of

Arminius to the faculty after his return in 1583 seem alto-gether inconsistent with the common account of his departure. Moreover, there is indubitable evidence that at the time Ar-minius went to Basel *nearly all the other students at Geneva left the city.* This fact has never before been alluded to in this connection. In the university register, kept by the rector, we find this entry : " Jacobus Arminius Veteraquinas. Theol. stud. ipsis Cal. Januarii 1582." After five more similar entries we come upon the following invaluable note, almost the only one in a roll of students covering more than three hundred years: "Anno 1582 Cal. Iulii regendæ scholæ pro-vincia in biennium proximum Anto. Faio iterum commissa est. *Eodem tempore, propter varios belli rumores et viciniam totam armis adversum nos trementem, studiosi fere omnes urbe cesserunt, paucique advenerunt.*" This precious record shows that just at the time of Arminius's withdrawal the university was nearly or quite suspended in consequence of the local wars. How interesting to find in this ancient register the names of Cromhout, Bysius, Brederodius, and Crucius, known to have been friends of Arminius at this time; also that of Adrian Junius (here written **Tjongius**), the law student with whom he afterward made his tour of Italy.

⁷ In the year 1622 the municipal government of Rotterdam erected in their chief market-place the bronze statue of Eras-mus, which one may still see in its place. He stands arrayed in his doctor's hat and toga, turning the leaves of the precious book which he helped to restore to the Church. If the ob-server can read Dutch he can decipher the following quaint inscription : "Here rose the great sun that set at Basel. May that imperial town honor and celebrate the saint in his tomb; the city that gave him birth gives him this second life. But the luminary of the languages, the spirit of morality, the glorious wonder that shone in charity and peace and divinity, is not to be honored by a mausoleum nor to be rewarded by a statue. Hence must the heavenly vault alone cover Erasmus,

whose temple scorns a more limited space." A smaller statue, also, adorns the house in which he was born, and which bears the felicitous inscription: "Hæc est parva domus, magnus qua natus Erasmus." Professor Tiele informs me that in the market-place, before the erection of the bronze, "there was a statue of sandstone, much damaged by the Spaniards. Among the Calvinists there was great indignation against this ' idol,' as they called it, and one of the Arminian preachers of the time, probably Hollingerus, wrote a humorous petition in which Erasmus calls upon the burgomasters and councilors to vindicate his ancient rights!"

⁸ Quite recently it has interested me to discover that the long before half-paralyzed but still active Thomas Lieber, in Latinized form Erastus, the father of the term though hardly of the doctrine of Erastianism, was at the time of Arminius's stay connected with the University of Basel, dying on the last day of 1583. Had Lieber taught all that Erastianism has meant in the history of the Dutch and English polemics, biographers of Arminius would find something very significant in this historical contact of the men from whom the terms Erastianism and Arminianism have respectively come.

⁹ In the library at Basel are still found two large volumes of unpublished letters written by the learned men of his generation to Grynæus. One of these epistles was written by Arminius in 1591, but I learned of its existence too late to have the pleasure of its perusal.

¹⁰ Polanus, an earnest disciple of Ramus, who afterward became a son-in-law to Grynæus, came to Basel in 1583, but whether in time to make the acquaintance of Arminius I do not know.

¹¹ Agrippa d'Aubigné, the illustrious sixteenth century representative of the family, had studied at Geneva before the

4

arrival of Arminius, but had run away, returning to France without permission in his thirteenth year. His romantic marriage was in 1583. After his final settlement in Geneva, in 1620, he was employed to complete the fortifications of the city, and was called to Basel to plan a new system of defenses for that place. He brought to Geneva an illegitimate son, whom he called Nathan Engibaud—Nathan, after the prophet sent by God to remind David of his sin, and as a perpetual reminder of his own; Engibaud, because this was irregularly and anagrammatically composed of the constituent letters of the family name, D'Aubigné. From this Nathan the Geneva family is descended, to which, by his grandfather's marriage, Dr. Merle, the historian, belonged.

[12] The memorable refugee colony of English Puritans, including Knox, Coverdale, Whittingham, and so on, left Geneva to return to their native land in 1560, the year of Arminius's birth. The official register of the colony, however, is still preserved in the archives of the *Hotel de Ville*. An interesting account of it may be seen in the *Bibliotheca Sacra* for July, 1862. Compare an article by Dr. Charles A. Briggs, entitled "An Ancient Type of Presbyterianism," in *The Independent* (New York), July 5, 1888. Arminius afterward encountered the Brownist refugees in Amsterdam.

[13] The eager interest with which Arminius first perused the writings of Ramus is not surprising. Milton was a more enthusiastic disciple than Arminius. Cambridge was alive with the new ideas. Bologna offered Ramus its Professorship of Philosophy. Nearly every Protestant university in Switzerland, Germany, and Holland had for years devoted adherents of "Ramism." The latest original monograph upon the system well says: "The true place of Ramus is at the head of the precursors of modern philosophy. . . . Ruining scholasticism, he every-where prepared the ways for a better philosophy."—Waddington, *Ramus, Sa Vie, ses Ecrits et ses Opinions,*

Paris, 1855, p. 897. Arminius discovered the incompleteness and the defects of the system sooner than most of his contemporaries.

¹⁴ The fine university building at Padua is the one in which Zabarella lectured and Arminius listened, having been begun 1493, and finished 1552. In these days it is worthy of mention that more than two hundred years ago, namely, in 1684, this university not only graduated a woman, Elena Lucrezia Cornaro Piscopia, but also erected a fine statue to her memory. It still stands in its place of honor at the right of the grand staircase.

¹⁵ From the university archives of Geneva it appears that Julius Pacius, who was Professor of Law 1580–1585, was also Professor of Philosophy 1582–1583. His abandonment of Romanism was about the time of his arrival in Geneva, and as he had previously studied and taken his degree in Padua it may have been through his influence that Arminius conceived so ardent a desire to sit at the feet of Zabarella. Many, however, thronged to Padua of their own accord from Protestant countries. Brandt says that when Arminius was there, *ipse quoque Germanos quosdam nobiles docuit Logicam.* (Page 30.) Pacius, and not his Spanish successor, must have been the one disturbed by the lectures of Arminius in the spring or summer of 1582.

¹⁶ The passage is as follows: "*Res admodum parva in magnum certamen excrevit apud principes artium Professores Jacobum Zabarellam et Franciscum Piccolomineum, qui acriter contenderunt, voce scriptisque, utrum via et ratio doctrinæ rectius procedat a rebus natura ipsa notis, an ab iis quæ nobis notæ sunt.*" In the same connection it was stated that three years before, which would be two years after the death of Jacobo, Sr., Zabarella had a quarrel with Petrella "*de rebus logicis,*" which "nearly broke up the university."

¹⁷ Two biographies of Arminius are published in America; the one a compilation by Dr. Nathan Bangs, published by Harper & Brothers, New York; the other, John Guthrie's translation of Brandt's Life of James Arminius, published by the Methodist Episcopal Church, South. Nashville, Tenn.

The churches in which Arminius preached in Amsterdam from 1588 till his election as professor at Leyden, 1603, are still standing and in use. By an anticipation, which I have never seen adequately noticed, the Dutch Reformed Church has always followed what Methodists would call "the circuit system" in all cities and towns having more than one congregation. Arminius, therefore, was never pastor of a particular flock. His marriage to Elizabeth Reael, daughter of a distinguished Amsterdam judge and senator, occurred in the *Oude Kerk* September 16, 1590. The house in which he here lived cannot now be determined further than that it was across the street from that of his friend, the Walloon or French Reformed pastor, Taffinus. At Leyden, when professor, he is believed to have resided on the Rapenburg Canal, near the university, and but a few rods from the house which has been identified as the one owned and occupied by the Pilgrim pastor, John Robinson, 1611–1625. It is interesting to know that James Arminius and John Robinson are buried in the same church. Readers who may desire light upon the relations in later time between the developed theology of the Pilgrims and the teachings of Arminius will find curious and instructive particulars from the pen of the present writer in McClintock and Strong's Cyclopedia, vol. x, art. "Theology, New England."

THE END.

BOOKS FOR CHILDREN

BY MRS. S. WORTHINGTON.

UNDER THE APPLE-TREES.

Illustrated. 12mo. Cloth.

Price..$1

A well-written story for children, and a story which inculcates excellent moral and religious lessons. It commends communion with Nature in her various moods, and shows how a beautiful religious character can be developed in the midst of unfavorable conditions. The perusal of the book cannot fail to make a good impression upon the minds and hearts of the young.—*Western Christian Advocate.*

THE SUMMER AT HEARTSEASE.

Illustrated. 12mo. Cloth.

Price..90 Cents.

A beautiful story for children. It relates how two little girls spent a joyous summer at home while their parents were traveling abroad for their health. The games they played and the stories told them are all very happily blended.

PHILLIPS & HUNT, Publishers; 805 Broadway, N. Y.

DESIRABLE BOOKS

BY THE

REV. JOHN M. BAMFORD.

FATHER FERVENT.

18 illustrations. 12mo. Cloth.

Price...**80 Cents.**

John Bamford is working along the same line as Mark Guy Pearse, and is doing a good work for English Methodism—the work of stirring up indifferent or backsliding Christians and encouraging the despondent. In this volume, which is the ablest, especially from the literary stand-point, in his entire list, he has appealed to class-leaders in particular to keep their vows, work out the plan under which they hold their appointments, and bless themselves in helping to keep alive the religious zeal of their fellow members. The story was written for English readers, whose system of church work is slightly different from our own, but it needs no alteration or interpretation to fit our own case. It is a powerful plea to those who almost "don't believe in class-meetings" and all that. As a story it is intensely entertaining. It brings together a group of characters whom it is a delight to meet. We commend the book to our class-leaders and to all Christian people who feel that they ought to be doing a little more than they are at present doing for the Master.—*Northern Christian Advocate.*

A tender, cheery, breezy book.—*Methodist Recorder.*

Comes before us with delightful freshness.—*Methodist Times.*

JOHN CONSCIENCE, OF KINGSEAL.

18 illustrations. 12mo. Cloth.

Price...**80 Cents.**

Those who have read *Elias Power, of Ease-in-Zion*, will know that *John Conscience* will be worth buying and worth reading, and worth lending to a friend who may not be able to buy one. Read it, and you will pray for a revival of old-time honesty, purity, and faithfulness.

Fresh and bracing. . . . One of the best books that could be placed in the hands of a young man entering on business.—*The Christian.*

ELIAS POWER, OF EASE-IN-ZION.

17 illustrations. 12mo. Cloth.

Price...**80 Cents.**

We know not who need to read it most—preachers or people. Perhaps if the pastor buys it first he will want to introduce it, and if the layman gets it first he will see that his pastor has it.—*Michigan Christian Advocate.*

Calculated to fire the heart of the sincere and to rebuke the formal and lukewarm.—*Sword and Trowel.*

PHILLIPS & HUNT, Publishers, 805 Broadway, N. Y.